How Toys Work

Screws, Nuts, and Bolts

Siân Smith

Heinemann
LIBRARY

Chicago, Illinois

www.capstonepub.com
Visit our website to find out more information about Heinemann-Raintree books.

To order:

☎ Phone 800-747-4992

💻 Visit www.capstonepub.com to browse our catalog and order online.

Edited by Dan Nunn, Rebecca Rissman, and Sian Smith
Designed by Joanna Hinton-Malivoire
Picture research by Mica Brancic
Production by Victoria Fitzgerald

Originated by Capstone Global Library Ltd
Printed and bound in China by South China Printing Company Ltd

16 15 14 13 12
10 9 8 7 6 5 4 3 2 1

Library of Congress Cataloging-in-Publication Data
Smith, Siân.
  Screws, nuts, and bolts / Siân Smith.
    p. cm.—(How toys work)
  Includes bibliographical references and index.
  ISBN 978-1-4329-6582-2 (hb)—ISBN 978-1-4329-6589-1
(pb) 1. Screws—Juvenile literature. 2. Bolts and nuts—Juvenile literature. 3. Toys—Juvenile literature. I. Title.
  TJ1338.S63 2013
  621.8'82—dc23   2011041311

Acknowledgments
The author and publisher are grateful to the following for permission to reproduce copyright material: © Capstone Global Library Ltd pp.8, 17, 22b (Lord and Leverett); © Capstone Publishers pp.6, 7 main, 9 inset, 9 main, 12, 13, 14, 15, 18, 19, 21, 10 inset, 10 main, 11 inset, 23 top (Karon Dubke); Shutterstock pp. 20, 5 (© Noam Armonn), 7 inset (© HomeStudio), 16 (© sonya etchison), 22a (© Nelstudio), 22c (© John Kasawa), 22d (© Tish1), 23 bottom (© HomeStudio), 23 middle bottom (© Jaroslaw Grudzinski), 23 middle top (© Taurus), 4 bottom left (© studio BM), 4 bottom right (© thirayut), 4 top left (© Piotr Sikora), 4 top right (© Noah Golan).

Cover photograph of toys made out of screws, nuts reproduced with permission of Shutterstock (© Gary Blakeley). Back cover photograph of a wrench being used on a nut reproduced with permission of © Capstone Publishers (Karon Dubke).

We would like to thank David Harrison, Nancy Harris, Dee Reid, and Diana Bentley for their assistance in the preparation of this book.

Every effort has been made to contact copyright holders of material reproduced in this book. Any omissions will be rectified in subsequent printings if notice is given to the publisher.

All the Internet addresses (URLs) given in this book were valid at the time of going to press. However, due to the dynamic nature of the Internet, some addresses may have changed, or sites may have changed or ceased to exist since publication. While the author and publisher regret any inconvenience this may cause readers, no responsibility for any such changes can be accepted by either the author or the publisher.

Contents

Different Toys

There are many different kinds of toys.

Toys work in different ways.

Screws

screws

Some toys use screws.

spiral

nail

screw

A screw is like a nail with a spiral wrapped around it.

screw

We use screws to hold things together.

spiral

screw

The spiral on a screw makes it hard to
pull out.

Screws hold this car together.

Screws hold this computer game together.

Nuts and Bolts

bolt

nut

Some toys use nuts and bolts.

Nuts and bolts hold things
together, too.

hole

hole

bolt

Two pieces have holes.

A bolt goes through the holes.

nut

A nut goes on the end of the bolt.
It holds the pieces together.

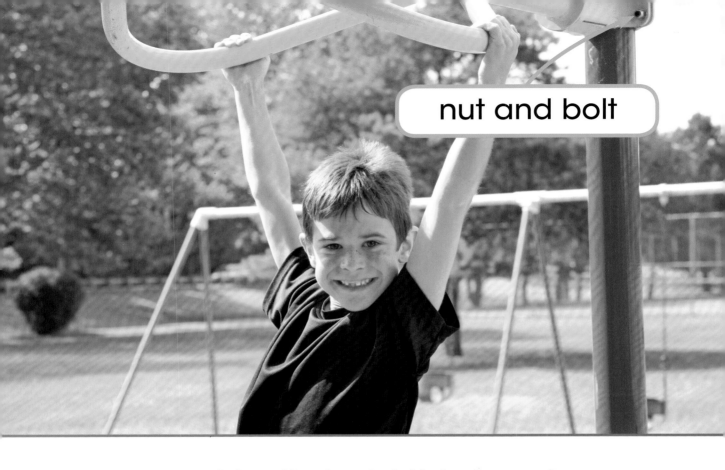

nut and bolt

Nuts and bolts hold this jungle gym together.

bolt

nut

Nuts and bolts hold this scooter together.

Turning

We have to turn a screw to push it in.
We have to turn a screw to pull it out.

We have to turn a nut to put it on
a bolt.

screwdriver

We use a screwdriver to turn a screw.

wrench

We use a wrench to turn a nut.

Quiz

a

b

c

d

Which one of these toys uses screws?

Answer on page 24

Picture Glossary

 bolt kind of thick screw with a flat end

 nut small piece of metal or plastic with a hole in it

 screw thin, pointed piece of metal similar to a nail. A screw has a spiral wrapped around it.

 spiral shape like a curl that winds around and around

Index

Answer to question on page 22: Toy b uses screws.

Notes for Parents and Teachers
Introduction
Show the children a collection of screws, nails, nuts, and bolts. Select children to pick out a screw, a nail, a nut, and a bolt. Label one example of each. What similarities and differences can they find between the nail, the screw, and the bolt? What do we use these things for?

More information about screws, nuts, and bolts
Explain that screws and bolts are different from nails because they have a spiral (or helix) shape wrapped around the outside. On a screw, this is called the thread. The thread on a screw means that you have to turn the screw to put it in something or take it out. A bolt is like a thicker screw, and most bolts have flat ends. Children can look at the thread on the end of a bolt and the thread inside a nut. They can then see how a nut can be put on a bolt to hold things in place.

Follow-up activities
Give the children the opportunity to experience how screws, nuts, and bolts can be used to hold things together. They could build or take apart models using a construction set. Show them how to use a screwdriver and wrench safely. For more advanced work on simple machines, children can work with an adult to discuss and play the games at: www.edheads.org/activities/simple-machines.

24